CONVERSATIONS

CONVERSATIONS

Bosede Funke Ademilua Afolayan

malthouse 𝒜𝒫

Malthouse Press Limited

Lagos, Benin, Ibadan, Jos, Port-Harcourt, Zaria

© Bosede Afolayan 2022
First Published 2022
ISBN 978-978-59447-5-4

Malthouse Press Limited
43 Onitana Street, Off Stadium Hotel Road,
Off Western Avenue, Lagos Mainland
E-mail: malthouselagos@gmail.com
Facebook:@malthouselagos
Twitter:@malthouselagos
Instagram:@malthouselagos
Tel: 0802 600 3203

International Distributors:
African Books Collective, Oxford, UK
Email: abc@africanbookscollective.com
Website: http://www.africanbookscollective.com

DEDICATION

To Him*
Who sits on the throne and,
Unto the Lamb,
Be glory, majesty, power
Honour, adoration and
Exaltation, forever
For the making of
Bosede Funke Ademilua-Afolayan
And to all those
Who need to discover themselves in the ultimate Source – God
The spring that never dries

* 26-7-2004

Son,

1. Son,
Roll out the drums
Strike the gong
The twin-*sekere* sound
And the *Gbedu* must boom
The *Gangan* tread masterly
While the tambourine
Break forth into a song
In praise of God: The maker

2. Our Earth

Red is the colour for battle
But our siege is over
Let's have blue for royalty
Our kings and love for
Our friends
Our world is green and
We must till the brown earth for a
Bounteous harvest

2

3. A moment of love

Wrapped in each other arms
Sleeping and waking
Breathing into each
Other's nostrils
Two hearts beating as
One
This moment to let go
A moment to love and give
A moment to make our world.

4. For us all

Everything around us
Is made for our good
The bad is in itself good
'If not this. What of the other'
The bitter pill to heal
Moving us higher
Gathering up the dust
With the seeds
As we move
On our way
Everything becomes
A pill and a life

5. I have a story to tell

Solo: I have a story to tell
Chorus: Tell. We are all ears
Solo: My story spins and spins and it falls on...
Chorus: Let it fall
Solo: It weaves and moves and falls on... Demilade

Demilade of the famed beauty
Golden-eyed; beautifully carved in their
Sockets: *Eleyinju ege*
Demilade of the imperial gait
Elenuiyo, the honey tongue
All men want Demilade
But she had other plans
Her face a permanent scowl
Her walk planned, purposeful
Like a soldier's

Once she was warned
'The way you carry on
You will not marry with
This frown of a face'
Demilade shrugged.
Demilade knew her onions
Focussed, she did not see any wall
Voluptuous, she grew beyond bounds
Spilling into the enemy camp

The Glass-ceiling
Does not exist
For Demilade
Our man-woman
Her frown fixed the
Girlish giggles of her peers

5

Up and higher she climbed
Blooming in the love
Silent encouragement of
Him whose
Footsteps she followed here

Then the descent
Like a flash. It all came crumbling
Like a pack of cards

Demilade missed the steps
With eyes opened
And it was not at night
The sun shone to guide
The moon to lead

But Demilade, the
Daughter of Abraham
The great cook
To whom household children
Run with empty plates
Could not...
She could not make
The *Egusi* soup she was famed
Demilade put her head between her laps.
The torrents open.

Demilade ran to her God

Midnight. Demilade reached out
Her hand fell on the Bible
Alone. She moved to source

Elderly worshippers saw
The queen and ran

6

Bewildered, Demilade fell
Like a log on the bare floor
She gave voice to her feelings

Relieved, Demilade sat
Like a wave the feeling
Fell again
Alarmed. Demilade looked
Into God's eyes
Could she see God?

Oro lo ba oro nile
Taa fi ba oka ninu oka
Oka kiin ma njo ka
Ohun to ju oka
Loka nje

Strange things abound
Behold corn in the python's stomach
Corn is no food for the python
Greater food is fit for the king

Friends and family dispersed
Alone with God
Demilade of the imperial gait
Rose and shone

How she did it
Its another story
Ojo lo palapa
To fi dohun
A mugun fewure

Torrential rain
Reduced the
Fortress to a
Debris rubble
That goats scale.

7

6. I have known pain*

Not at the deliberate
Pinch(ing) of restless fingers

Not that which results
In the turning and turning
Of the change
In the face of the moon or
of that first meeting
And of the pains and joys
Of a new birth

I have felt pain
At the movement of life
When my loved one
Moved on

I have seen pain
Mirrored at Judas' kiss
That sold me into slavery
I have known pain
The pain of living
Amidst fences of men
Yet alone

But this pain
Is deeper
Deeper than you can feel
My body writhes in its pool
My face contorted
The agony of our own life

---

* 23-5-2004. First published in Sandra Grayson (Ed.) *Langston Hughes Harlem Renaissance.*

8

Of our own making
I have seen pain
Written in bold letters
On the face of women and children
Displaced. Desolate. Deprived

I have heard their singing
Sorrowful songs seeping
Through walls
Sweeping seas
Scaling heights
Blown into our souls

I can feel their pain
A handful and a bunch
On their head trekking
To nowhere
This pouch they carry
Could this be all for them?

My heart bleeds
For orphans
Condemned to a bleakness
Not of their making

I look at the album of our recent past
The page flicks open
To reveal the carnage
Of Ife and Modakeke

I open the book
To encounter
The despoliation of Odi
That of Aguleri and Umuleri
Idiaraba of Lagos
The war of Warri
The case of Kano and Kaduna

9

The archives burst
With records of Operation
Wet of the Wild Wild West
And the state of emergency of '62

Now, before our very eyes
The Sahara rests uneasy
While the plateau burns
Oh! The acrid smell of hot
Human flesh like barbecue
In the oven of ignorance
Wither Nigeria?

I block my ears
To the cries of the many
Our full graves burst at the seams
The things my eyes have seen
The things my ears have heard
My soul wells up within me
My eyes; a lake of tears
With many other voices
I cry:
PEACE

7. Glory*

Glory be to God for painful relationships
For a Cain whose countenance must fall
A Judas to sell us
For just 30 pieces of shekels
We cannot choose our relations nor our followings
Thank You, dear God
For Joseph's kins
I give You, praise for this sweet-pain

---

* 18-7-2004

8. All Brain

A Head
16 cows for a Head.
Who owns a Head?
Who allows a head?
The foot hits a stone
Not a head!
'A kii beru ori
Ka fi fila de idi'
Who's afraid of the head
To cap a buttock?
A Head is a head
Not a bowl
Not a sacrifice
For ablution
The spits
The sneers and
A tray bearing cowries
But a head is a head, sir!

9. My own

 it is yours
It is mine
Nkem is mine
Temi is Nkem
Onome is Temi
We are one.

God made our country, but
Men and Women
Moulded walls
After their hearts
And their gods

God gave us all
Trees
Waters
Fruits
Intellect
Imagination
What is man? To set limits
For another, equally born
Diverse breeding
God, only God
He alone'

10. Thou art Woman

What mother
Leaves her pink bundle
In a trash can
For the dogs and hyenas
Of this world?

What woman
Leaves her child
On a slope and
Tells the cars of this world
To race her down?

'Fire burns hard'
The woman shakes hers first
Who shakes off the daughter's?

Child; you are light
Left beside darkness
Your youth and ignorance
A pawn for the women.

14

11. The Chamber

We are the women
We are the world
Cocooned all
In our embrace
We can heal the world

Captive
Legs pulled in
 A foetus struggles

Emerged
To the fold of waiting-women
'Welcome'
We greet you
You have tried
We have waited
For this hour
Take
Take
Take
Gifts of our world
Trapped.

But for the love of the Father
She rose again
Multitudes rose with her

They are here
The Women
Eagle-eyed

They have come
Enough!

15

Let it be
F or our world
For our sakes

12. Bruised

I've been bruised and battered
I've been crowned with thorns
I've been lain down and crossed
A mark has been laid:
Beware all:
Drive her away
Anyone who sees her:
Brutalise.
Humiliate.
Take.
Use.
Dump.
'The child of a king, is no meat for the hyenas'

In all
Like a sheep led to the slaughter
I did not open my mouth

I have drunk vinegar
Cow-urine and a
Mixture of
'I-do-not-know-what'

I have eaten
All kinds
Herbs and spinach
Food and medicine

I have fought the good fight with words
In silent supplication
With the body
In fasting and abstinence

17

I have struggled
Against odds
Just for a place in the sun

When I remember
'that the man dies in all who keep silent'
I open my mouth
The Engineers are at work
I shake as leaf
Blown by the autumn wind
I am silenced.

Each time I am pushed back
Hmmh.
Shooed like an offending chick
Hmmh.
When a goat is pushed
To the wall …
To the wall …
A cow without a tail lives in Sabongida
But it has a creator

The fly eats man
But when man eats the fly…

When I close my eyes
In total anguish
When my heart breaks
At this load
This burden I carry
When I look for help
And I am met with
Blank stares and
Total neglect

18

In open amazement
I stand.
Confused.
In anger,
I retreat.
In disgust. Insouciant
I marvel at man's ways
The way of our world.

But each time
I stepped out
Bright colours of rainbow
Decorate my sky
The howling wind gives way
To the cool breeze
The sun and moon,
Day and night,
Break into Joy!
With each move
The heavens sing
The joyous song of
Halleluyah .

13. Bruised Again*

Bruised.
 Sore through
Laid on the slaughter slab
Butchered like a cow.

A couch for a bed
A table for an exam
Or a dissecting
A caesarean
Legs strapped to a pole
Hung apart
A barbecue or
A sacrifice!
Huge sun glared
Strung to little seeds of light
Stood high up as chandeliers
A huge bulb glared
Into the intestine
A hand poked
Searching
Rummaging in the blood
A gloved-hand in red
Drips on.

---

* 4 – 4 - 91

14. Harvest Time

I sang in Igbo
Chukwukeluka answers:
You have been here

I tried Hausa
Ubangiji said:
One has been here
In your name
Oghene says:
Look inwards child
'I made a rapid dialogue with my legs'
Back to base
I looked into my heart

Abasi calls out:
Forgive, child
The vegetable is eaten by
The insect that grows with it, child,
We see you
Everywhere
Let the wheat and weed grow
Harvest time will tell.

15. A Desire*

It is my desire
And my wish
To worship you
And to honour your name

So I left my fishing nets
I abandoned all
To seek your face

I held on to your garment
In life
In spirit
With faith
For a double portion
Of your power.

And I walked on water!

With my eyes
Fastened on you
Author and Finisher
Alpha and Omega
Unwavering
Like Abraham
I staggered not in unbelief

You live in my reflection

---

* 5-5-2004

22

I open my mouth
To declare you
Yet I allow another
The use of my mouth

And thrice before
The cock's crow
I denied you.

Not to save me
But in ignorance.

Above all
You insist:
'On this rock
I'll build my church'

16. If you see me

If you see me
Going on a lonely road
Muttering to myself:

Do not fear for my soul
I am not lost
I am looking for me.

Constrained like Sizwe
I have died severally
To rise many times
Like Orpheus I find myself
And assume my name
A beauty from the ashes

Do not be alarmed.
I may mutter
I am talking to Him
Who sees me
Who listens always.
Aletikara bi ajere

24

17. On Our Father s Love

To what can we compare a mother's love
In pain she hid me
In pain she pushed me out
Into her joy
A father's love is greater
On this we rest.

The father's investment
Yields bountifully in a child
On our father's love
We rely
What love can compare
To that whose life
Gave meaning to mine
Who laid His life
A ransom for my soul
Your love redeemed me.

This debt I pay:
With my praise

18. Dance*

Sounds of vibrant *gangan*
And *sekere* sounds within
Dan dan da

Arise
Rise with the sun
Up from your slumber
To the light of God
Dance and rejoice
It's your day of Joy
Praise Him
Whose love invests
Life into your being
Rejoice in His mercies;
New each day.

_____

* 29-7-2004

19. Combat

Arms ready
In combat
Like a boxer's
Left and Right
Punches fly
Fencing
Dodging
Bending
Trashing under a cover
An *aran*: A cocoon or A maze
Aso etu: Clothe an Elder
Demands wisdom from its wearers
Alone in the ring
Fenced by hyenas
Bruised and Brutalised
The foes are fallen and
I lay my arms
Reaching out for the
Cooling satisfying relief of
Water.

20. Who?

Who will celebrate
A woman?
Who will roll out the
Drums
For an Eve?
Who will sing the praises
Of a woman?
Who will hero-worship
A lady as Lady Macbeth.
The priestess is disdained
Even in her land.
Even witches are women
As Mary, the mother
A virgin with child
Bearer of the seed
For the sins of the world
This seed
That lives with us
In us
A daily celebration waits

21. Be bold

Be strong, my darling be bold
As I rule the waves
Hover around the world
As a bird flutters
Nowhere to perch
Your heart, my darling, my home.

22. Here we are

By this river
We sat and sang
When problems like the wind
Flung us in millions
We hastened out of our bodies.

How can we sing songs of victory
In chains
In a strange compound

Your love was the straw
 That gave our soul a
Name and a body
We held on
Carried by the torrents
We clutched to it
This love that defends as
No sword can.

23. In days like these

In days like these
Men are better
Without a heart

We see them
As they are
 Brutish Beasts
Calculating Cains
Sticky fingers
Sweeping others' blessing
As they play and
Steal and manoeuvre

Men have refused
To be men
Men are reduced
To beasts
In an orgiastic display of
Sheer animalistic impulse
Not to tame
But to destroy
In a show of power.

24. I am

I am Moremi
From palace to raffia
In the prison
Chained in the enemy camp
Turning to save
A race.

I am the tongue
Whose fires blaze
The dark places

I am Atunbi
In mother's womb again?
Born of the water
Born of the spirit

I am the light
Shine bright for all to see
Light; even at evening time

25. Tempest Tossed

'When upon life's billows
You are tempest tossed '
As when a sudden hail storm
On the wings of the whirlwind
Your sight clouded
Your raised hands
To shield your eyes
Steadily you stood
Do not for once
Think all is lost
In the valley
Wallowing in the deep
On the land
On the mountain
Riding the waves as horses
 A hand is raised
To steady your fall
Even while you stumble
Receive strength
Back and better
To face more storms
Armed with the past
You in Him.

26. The Song of an Undergraduate

I am now the master of me.
I do with me as I please
I roam in shorts and
Cross in mini-skirts
With chains fit for dogs
As belts to strain
My sagging trousers
I show my backside
To erring eyes
I draw stares
I couldn't care less
I saunter on
Airs self-created
I see not mother's tears
I bar my ears
To father's words
I am but me and
One
I forget:
Freedom has its rules.

27. Game-Master

I sing this song to you
In whose hands.
I am a pawn
In deft strokes
Defiant.
You moved me
Cover for others in shade
Laid up: standing in the gap.
You made me
A wheel to wind
At your wish
There is but one life
One life to live
No time for frivolities
No room for trifles
When bigger issues
Stare us in the face
Our energy we lay waste
On the altar of
Who's right?
Who's wrong?
When finer issues
Of life remain on ice.

28. And He rested

For six days He worked
Striving and moulding
The porter feverishly worked
His mind; a turbulence:
To bake.
To roast.
To wrought and
To traverse
A whirlwind unable to rest.

He tilled many farms
Like the Harvester brought
Many seeds home

On the 7th day
He took His rest
Found His rest
In me
His trust; His love.

29. The true life

Solid gold in bars of pound and dollars
Riches beyond man's imagination
Wardrobes full bursting at the seams
Imports from Italy
Perfumes of Arabia and the Egyptians arts
The oil of Nigeria and the
Peoples of this world
Automobiles as legs
Flying on wings of machines
Trophies of silver and
Bronze, man's exploits
Learning in scientific
And aesthetic philosophies
A man without God
Is but shreds.

30. Ours to Roam?

Ours was a free field
To roam and romp
In sheer ecstasy and splendour of our maker
Before HIV/AIDS tethered
Many to a stake
'Go! Multiply
Fill the face of the earth'
It was a charge
To both great and small
And lust lurks in the
Deep recesses of the high and low
Promiscuity its art
Mistresses as concubines
Bastards its manifestation?
Who dares call one a Bastard?
Everyone was fathered by one
Cocooned in a womb.
Many a renegade on beds
Of honour conceived
Yet stolen waters
Can be sweet
Bearing vital seeds
For other lands and clans
Seeds of future feud.

31. Architecture of Fear

Round and round we turn
In circles of hate and
Buck-passing
Pointing fingers
Hands ready to war
Fists hard in battle
Nostril flaming red
Its hair in a dance of rage
Higher and higher
We built our castles of hate
Homes?; 'Architecture of fear'
Yet God in His infinite mercies
Endowed us with all things
Including: Love and fairness.

32. Open up*

Open your eyes
Open your mind
To behold
The wond'rous ways of God.

Open your hearts
To receive Him
Open the door
Let Him come in

For a long time
The gates were locked
Barred to the king's entry
By ignorance
By nonchalance
The veil beclouded the view
Of the glorious light.

Now
Listen to him
AS he knocks
Silently
In great trepidation;
Yet in all His splendorous power
He hesitates
Looking for that moment
The moment which
In a flash
He can recognise

---

* 25-9-2004

The love you owe him
He knocks timidly still
Silently. Again and again
Calling and waiting
To let Him come in

Open your eyes
To His manifold blessings
Daily He loads you
With all good things
Open up!
Let the king of glory come in.

33. You are me

You are one long river
Of black and white stripes
A Zebra in the flowers
And green of our land
The tom-tom sounds
Calling a stop;
Make way
Your waters flow
Through the ages
In an ancient time
First of the black
The long winding
Uncharted stretch
Melting the white stripes
Flowing into the Benue
Into the Niger;
The Male,
The female
The food and the water
The water and the fire
To light and blaze the way
To consume the shaft and the weed.
To cool parched throats
To chart the way for our peace.

The drum sounds again:
Tom. Tom. Tom. Tom.
Its resonant voice
Searching our soul
Reaching to its depth
Turning eye to eye:
'Each one turn to the other'
Let the eyes meet the eyes

On both sides of the table
No longer in a combat
But in a fresh recognition:
You are my blood
The bone of my bone
The cell of my blood
The DNA confirmed it
It is in your look
Your gait. Your choices
Your eyes ...
You are me.

34. A song*

I wished I could dance again

Once, my dear
The whole world was
A dance-ground for me
Every beat was music
In my ear
In my soul
And I would dance!

Father's Reduvison
His gramophone
Played all night
All day
All for me

The beating of tins
Its rattle was music
Father pegs the yams leaves
Each stroke driven in the soil
"Was he pounding yam"
The movement itself was a dance
To draw my feet out

The pillars, the roof, the lintels
All break forth in song for me
And I would dance
Not in reckless abandon
But in sheer pleasure

---

* 15-01-2004.

Refrain: Let me dance
     Let me dance
     While I am young
     When I grow
     Who knows
     Tomorrow may refuse me,
    A dance.
    Let me dance
     While I am young

Women; wrappers on their breasts
By the hearth
Small talk, peeling melons
Suddenly burst into a song:
"Where is she?
Let her come
This lady from Lagos
Dance a little for us"

In all innocence, cheerfully
With all joy, I would dance...

But, they watched and waited.

The male-stone is busy
On the flat face of its female
The squishing song
Like a child's foot in a wet shoe
Its rhythm draws a note

But here she comes.
"Stop singing.
The pepper is wet with your saliva
This song is too much"
Your song wakes everyone
From this village even to Lagos
You sang your way through.

45

We know. Not Aduke but Ajoke
Had a dip in the river
The neighbouring shrubs foam painted.
A dip in the tub
Under His showers
My daily bath, a ritual of songs and dance
A communion. Naked in God's presence.

Here . A moment of no shame
A time of atonement with Him; my maker
Each morning
A return to the beginning
"Naked in His presence"

Each stroke of the sponge and soap
Each flush and splash
The trickles caressing my trunk
A song is made to Him; who made me
Tales are told of great men
Stripped. Arrested for life
Just at that moment
The moment of truth
The naked moment
In the bath
Not me, for
"Naked I come"

My weakness is my strength
By your loving kindness.
Time draws on
Things are coloured now
Could the music be lost?

Refrain: Let me dance while I can
For tomorrow
May make days longer

With its tales of joys and sorrow
But once a song is woven into my steps
I can, even in sadness and pain
Draw a song and a hope.

35 At the Edge.*

At the edge of this cliff
We stand.
To fall or fly
Or back trot
To dance the music of yester years
To sink or swim
At the bank of
The river of life.

We cling to memories of yesterday
We hesitate:
"To be or not to be"
To soar or succumb
We prevaricate.

But we are edgy now for a choice
At this edge
That makes or mars us

Like Tom and Jerry
Caricatured Adults
We lay waste our energy
Life is more than winning arguments
All of the time.

Or more like Jimmy and Alison
Looking back always in anger
Is life not more than bickering?

---

* 07-02-2004

48

Choose now;
A crutch or a wing
Choose.

I choose to look up
I choose life not HBP
I choose to rise above the circumstances of life
I choose to rise with the morning.

36. I know He s Concerned.*

Many days I hurt
My heart cries out
My soul bleeds from aching.

On my bed
I trash around
Fighting for my life
Against a cold or a fever
My head aches
Migraine blinds my sight
I seem not to see
So, I rest my head on Him
My lips too thick even to pray

My soul holds on
I stay focused on Him
His words borne on the wings of breeze
Convey sweet sounds into my ears:
"The gates of hell shall not prevail"
He says:
"You may travail
Since you live with them
Hold on,
You will prevail"
These words like the balm of Gilead
Reassure my aching soul.

Many days, tension rises so high as a wall
Built on blocks of bickering
With animosity as rooftop

———————————————

* 04-05-2004

The air tensed
You could cut hatred with a blunt knife.
I seek solace in silence
I sit.
With arms folded
I ask Him to take charge

Terrible times may come
I may have asked
"Where are you, God?"
I may have looked up
"God, are you still there?"

At such times
I seek a soul mate to whisper,
God loves you, girl.

In all these
I have never said
God is not concerned
God has not abandoned me
Like some mothers, their babies
Never. Ever.
For I know
His eyes are on the sparrows
He feeds the lilies
He is concerned about me
Who He has made in His image
He is not too busy
His network is ever open
To answer my call.
He is concerned.

37. If You Like.*

If you like
Beat me into a pulp
In a moment
When fury veils your vision
When rain of angry fists
Make rapid but calculated
Falls to break me, spirit and soul.

If you like
Let words like daggers
Fall into my naked torso
As I lay helpless.
Coals of abuse
Burn my heart
Thoughtless torrents of words tumble down
Seeping recklessly into the pores of my skin
My body shudders
At this strange invasion
Your vehemence rudely
Hammers them into" the castle of my skin"
An unwelcome stranger is repelled
And manifest in bumps sprains, and bags
I cover up with a smile
I walk about like a zombie

If you like
Turn me into a rind
Thoroughly sucked and spent
Discarded on the dung hill.

---

*03-10-2004

If you like
Crowd my mind with images of horror
While I struggle in the maze of negative spirits
If you like
Bake me in the furnace of your fury and
Sting my soft senses in a barrage of hateful words
Teni be igi loju, igi aruwe
A little rain,
A little sunshine
Even the dirt as manure
I will grow again.

38. If I Must Stay.*

If I must stay
Stay, then it must be.
When tradition demands
Filial attachment orders
Agape calls:
Men must obey.

If I must stay
It will not be
Like a bear tied to a stake.
Harangued.
Spat on.
Tortured.
Tormented.
Surrounded by hungry hounds
Waiting to devour.

If I must stay
Let it be on my terms
If not
Let the parting shot be:
Each man to his tent,
God for us all

---

* 10-10-2004

54

39. **Last Night.***

Only last night
I dreamt.

Yes, I dreamt
Not of myself
Not of my life
Not of my work
So, don't give up yet

Yes, I dreamt
Of my country,
My dear mother land
And my father land, too.

Don't laugh yet
Don't give up on Nigeria

Dreams are real and
I choose to see
Nigeria great again
Dreams are true
Nebulous manifestations of fears
Played out in Nightmares?
Choose what you wish.

But I choose to see hope
Like Obasanjo once
I see hope
Yes.
I choose life.

---

*   16-10-2004

Last Night
Jehovah granted me a vision of a land
"Where no man is oppressed"
Because of creed or colour, sex or tribe
Where bickering, backbiting and battles cease
Where the Aguleris and the Umuleris
The Ifes and the Modakekes
The Ijaws and the Itshekiris
Mingle and intermingle peaceably

Then Odi will not shed blood and
A force reduced a town to rubbles
But in brotherhood we shall stand
Where Clark's voice rings out:
"Hear each other speak
See the face in a crowd"
I choose to see
A land of people powered
By the right values
Schools open pushing out minds
Readily absorbed into
The waiting arms of the Naira
Racing well with the Euro, Dollar and Pound

I choose to see
Nigeria making permanent friends
With permanent dynamic interest
A small still voice warns
"There is no Eldorado
The leopard cannot change its pores"
Nigeria tottering at over half a century
Fastened in strained fellowship
Can any good come out of Abuja?

We are what we decide to be
We can make Heaven of hell
Don't ask me how
W .H Auden proffers:
"Poetry makes nothing happen"
It may be only a dream or just poetry
And I choose to dream.

40 A Song for A Season.*

And What More Can I Say.
Remember;
The man who was pushed into a river
Populated by giant carnivorous crocodiles
And he swam in fury
To the shore.

How did he do it?
You ask me.

Remember;
The young man whose life depended
On the walk of his life saddled with an open glass of water
To reach the end of a kilometre
A kilometre that seemed like an eternity
And the water did not spill

His left was paved with sympathisers urging him on
Plying the glass with sweet soothing words
And to the right
A kerb of destructive critics
Loading the cup with vituperations
He got to the end

How did he do it?
His eyes on the course
Wavering neither to the left nor to the right
He trudged on in earnest
Fearing neither foe nor friend.

———————————————

* .11-05-2003

Remember;
The donkey whose owner gave up on it
"You are no good"
He dug a hole
Alive, he buried it.
Like a lamp led to the slaughter
It opened not its mouth
It stood silent shaking off the sand on its back
And, at each movement
The dirt goes under
And becomes the pedestal shooting him
Out of the grave.

What more shall I say?
For time would fail me
To tell of Abraham, and of Hannah
Of Thomas Edison, and of Abraham Lincoln
Time would not permit.

41. You Were Abiodun
A Poem for Late Professor Abiodun Adetugbo

You were Abiodun
You arrived on a festive day
Amidst pomp and pageantry
"Christ is Born"

You could have left for this journey
On any other day
But you chose a Christmas day
"Christ is Born"

It is said;
You asked for a packed luggage
To embark on this journey
You believed "*kaiyetoro*" was not home
That home lies beyond
They say, Abiodun has cheated death many times
Oh. The medical diagnoses: Too many
You beat all
To willingly lay down your life on a bed
And wake into eternity
"Christ reigns"
Adieu, Professor.

42. If Men Were Wine*

If men were wine
Women would taste
To see which is vintage or stale
Or which would last till the end
The fluffy foam that draws one on
To come, come and taste.
Wives would run from the dirt
 That makes the murky base
And would go on to
Taste others and see
Which would endure till the night
And savour, and linger on
At the sweetest of all
Making stories over
The inexplicable touch and taste
Of the wine on the lips
Just at that moment and to
Pray, stay, stay forever

---

* 17-12-2004.

43. Even Jesus Walked

If the fog is a cover
For a maze of a mind
The soul like a shuttle surreptitiously sails to and fro
In an amazing loom without an end
The cloud is heavy
The heart, too
Like a woman heavy with child
The body at war with itself
The soul travels as referee
The bed now an arena
Turning and tossing in a ceaseless dance
Of torturing thoughts

The release begins with a step
A prayer
A purpose
A push and
A lifting.

44. Give Me A Reason*

Give me a reason
Why you make me cry so.

Give me a reason
For your neglect

Give me a reason
While I toil to train
Wobbling under a heavy load of burden
Lightened only by Him
Give me a reason
Why I shouldn't say: goodbye

Is there a reason?
Physically entwined yet souls apart
We grope.
So near yet so far
To find a meaning
To this play, this life
You say:
"I am trying my best"
Your best isn't enough for me
For it is nothing
And you know it.

You have no reason.

---

* 30-10-2003

45. A Wife's Prayer

God, give me a clear mind
A deep, discerning one
To accommodate
Even the stupidest idea

God, grant me that peace
The peace of mind to admit
Even the wrong I never committed
Not to claim any right even when I am right.

God, give me the energy
To earn a living
Be a house keeper and a cook
A lover and a mother
All at once.

To know where my husband's
Ties, socks and handkerchiefs are
When he asks for them
And to pair the socks up
So, he won't have to wear a red and a blue to work
All at once.

46. Remember Lot's Wife?

Lot's wife was a woman of like passions
Our wants and needs
All anxieties of life
Food to eat and money for clothes
Children to carry on

We dare not look back
No. Not once

We are the salt to sweeten
Not a pillar of salt
Left to the vagaries of the elements
A monument of waste
We must rest the battle daggers
Warring in our heads
And choose
The way
The life
The light
The truth.

47. Dead Stories

There are some dead stories
As dead as dead could be
They are the stories of "if you had"
Tales of "Had it been," "If you did"

Dead stories are what they are
They remain dead and buried
Excavated by story tellers of failure
"I could have helped but..."
"Had I known..."
Stories of regret

Stories manufactured in retrospect
"Looking back now..."
"There would have been..."
"If only you had listened..."
"If you did not..."
Now, you didn't
So, what shall we do?

Sing to me a new song
A story of action
I did this
At the crucial time
I stepped in
Like a lion
I played this note
A tale of courage and chivalry
Beat into music songs of bravery
Of a Chaka championing the occasion
Of that intervention at the nick of time

Let it rise into a crescendo
The high tone of the praise of those
Who against all odds staked their lives
Laid it on the line
For a life for a soul

Weave into music for me
A song in praise of little kindness
When it was most needed
And the world dances in praise
Of God for help at a time of need
Draw a beat from the movement of my feet
As I dance in honour of Him: my Helper.

48. CAPTIVE

You are your own enemy
Tethered by your tongue
Slave to your own doings
A victim of your own undoing
Betrayed by your mouth

Ignorant and veiled
You did not see the pit
And you walked in
But like Joseph
It is well even in the well.

The lawful captive can be set free
The eagle among the chicks
Will yet find its heights
When the falcon hears the falconer

49. This Sea of Life

The sea surges forward
Its silvery surface summons
Deceptively alluring at its low ebb
We close in
Its high tide eats our monuments

Like Jonah on a trip to Tarshish
Ends in the belly of the fish
Moses adrift on the water
Finds himself in the palace
Arnold sees it all on Dover Beach:
"Let us be true to ourselves"

The sharks and the whales are waiting
So, darling, let us flow in this stream of life
With the spirit of God as our guide.

50. On Small Mercies in Lagos

I woke up this morning
And a song of praise issue forth from within me
At dawn, I was still in bed
A wonder.

On the wings of thought
I raced back to Isolo
Sleeping and waking like cock
The car was a mobile house
The torture of traffic to Yaba
The evening was a nightmare
Of endless search for water
What a life.

I heaved a sigh,
Purring like an over fed cat
I snuggled into the sheets
And sang my heart out
For this small mercy
In praise of Him
Who has put a new song in mouth.

51. EXODUS (1988)

Composite dung
Land of many contradictions
Sprawling sinuosities of architectural maze
A robber's den. Old England reincarnated.
No progenitor of the scalded-body
But a child of Baba Dudu
The "soulless trunk" finds succour in you...My land

I am not going to chant the song of Jodughatu
I am not going to herald the end of time.

Bang . We must be deaf to that sound
It is the fiery GIANT clamping down on Mr Short
He has been dwarfed mute
Pores; outlets of his body cemented
Metabolic activity will not occur here
Soot, toxic waste mingle daily here with him
A living-dead torso rolls down our Campus quarters

Do not say I told you it is the furious kick of the heavy boot
Do not say I said it is the pestle pounding the man ...or the baton?

The bandwagon knocks on your door
The four-wheel is hooting
The commuter-bird of the sky awaits your arrival
Your wings poised ready for flight
Are you the bird perched on the apex of the leaf
Waiting for the stone from our Big Brother
That will catapult you into motion?
Like Andrew, like the dove and Columbus
The Pilgrim Fathers seek a paradise.

71

The green light has beckoned
The answer is this exodus.

Look up the sky
The clouds are heavy
Will the water whirl down as rain
Or fade away in this heavy hectic brain drain?
Look out,
The land is alarmed
But who startled it?

They say this space is occupied
They say the sky is full
They say it is an Excess Zone
Redolent of chest-beating men
No matter how tall they walk
It is still on the land

72

52. In Memoriam*
To the late Prof E. A. Babalola

Ethereal pencil of light
Flashed on the back cloth
Of this auditorium
Your head like wool among the sea of black heads
The heavy cloud bore down
Your feet dragged on like Elesin-Oba's
Drugged by the cold hands of death
Eyes opened, seeing all
Mute at man's ways
You were here. Yet, not here.

* 26-6-2004

53. In Memoriam 2
For Adebisi Ademola Ademilua, Jan 23 1979 – Dec 23rd 2010

You walked into that darkness
I searched and searched
You had mingled with the dark night
I peered hard, my eyes hurt
From too much straining
I called out, but you did not hear
My heart went out to you and
My heart bleeds still.

The vacuum your leaving created
Too big for any to fill, you
Touched a life here, you
Gave a word of encouragement, you
Paid through the nose
That some may live, you
Endured lonely nights in strange lands
Through Jo'burg
In Heathrow, Gatwick
To Berlin, in Dubai, to Senegal
You traversed and sojourned
Like the eagle, you flew in
Those man-made machines in the skies
There were turbulences in those troubled flights
Yet, you did not fall
You came back each time
With stories and your hands bearing souvenirs of those lands.

And then,
Only to sleep
To wake crawling like a toddler!
And then,
Before we could close our eyes in prayer
You LEFT.

You left,
But not your kindness
Nor your love and care
Your helping hands at all times
Are left
And bear witness
That you were too good
"The good does not last"
So you came,
Like a comet and flashed
Through our lives.
Life has visited on us
Yet, one of its contradictions

I am lost in the mysteries of God
Your departure conceals for me
Illuminations which God alone
In His infinite knowledge can
Transform into gratitude
But in all, through the eyes of faith
I give thanks.

54. This Academic Obstacle

Based on a poem 'An Obstacle' by Charlotte Perkins Gilman
(1860-1935)

I was in a hurry
Almost at a frenzy to finish
A paper that needed to be done
There were so many things
Demanding my attention
Other people's papers to read
If let unattended at that time
May ground my own
A little squabble
Fuelled by tactlessness
Could have wrecked
My emotions and delayed
If not for God

I pushed that behind me
There were so many things
To read & write
To type & proofread
To photocopy
To document
To revise
To edit
And a class to teach
An appointment to keep
As there was a deadline.
In the hurry
I was blind
To the glass-blocking my way
Waiting and watching
I ran into it
Headlong

It was so thick
I couldn't see myself
Beyond this barricade
But it stood still and strong
Cutting me off and out
'You have no inheritance here'

I close my eyes to it
I refused to see it
A goal has been set
This work must be done
I've been stretched thin
With this load I carry
I did not acknowledge
Even when I saw:
 A closed door at 5 0'clock
A huge iron barricade
Tell-tale of non-admittance
And of course, again
A bureaucratic network
Of letters, memo and instructions
Who is a secretary to outwit a boss
With the milk of human kindness!
I knew what I was in for
In that instance I saw
The glass welled up like a huge
Fire in the harmattan
I saw myself between the
Devil and the deep blue sea

Going seemed impossible
Retreating suicidal
Like Moses I was
Between the Red Sea
And the Egyptian chariots
I hesitated

The options were open
Give up and cry.
That's typical.
You could negotiate:
Analyse and rationalise
Be tactful and win
This glass stood unyielding.
Backed by authority
Armoured by protocols
Rules that I could not bypass
Even in Hague.

With an Elias and an Ajibola
An Akinyemi may come to judgement
I could rouse Cessario of Esa Oke
From his slumber if I like
With fluency and articulate construction:
A mind has been set
A strong will cannot be broken.

I had wept profusely
I had begged foolishly
My knee-cap may stick to the floor
I had insisted on truth
I could have been speaking
To a deaf wall
The handwriting on the wall:
'You have no place here'

In obstinate fury and helplessness
I let open the floodgate of words
The angry words tumbled down
Surprised faces like cracked walls
Gaped wildly at me
'So, she could talk'
Inflamed by the ignorance

78

That anger is a natural response
Like a leaking basket
I let down angry words
Hitherto repressed in the unconscious
That only thickened
The glass the more.

My eyes cleared
I recalled my strength
I affirmed my right as His child
Openly I sang 'All is well"
I am too connected to God
To be frustrated
Not by man
Not by man-made rules or passion

For I know that
With God and I on this journey
I am a conqueror
 And I walked through this glass as if it wasn't there
How did the glass dissolve?
It's not for me to ask Him.

55. Forget me

You said I should forget about you
That you are gone, and gone forever
And, that I should move on
But I say:
How can I forget?

When you are always in my mind
I see you in my sighs and in my silences
I see you in life's little things and big things
I see you when I am by myself

Surrounded by a crowd
But none sees my face
I see you in my highs and in my lows
I see you in my adversity
I behold your face in my joys
What you would have done for me
What you did for me
"Memory is master of death"

How could I forget your brotherly love?
When others saw a nobody
You wrote of the inspiration I had been to you
When many saw failure; you stood by me
Oh, how I miss your prayers
Oh, how I miss …

The creator made you because of me
I lost you in the hustle of life
In trying to accomplish
I forgot the little things that make up life
I believed you would be well
Well, I forgot to pray

80

To Him who created you
Could my prayers have kept you on this side?
And, I lost a treasure in my forgetfulness
How can I forget?

The world says:
No one is indispensable
I have found that to be so untrue
No one has been able to fill your shoes
How can I forget?
It is the nature of man to remember
Memory and remembering will continue
As long as lice are on the head
The nails will be soiled by blood
Man will always recollect, for the elephant never forgets
How can I forget?
Tell me.

56. In Your Hands*

I take my destiny in my hands
And I stand against all and
Everything that hinders my growth
My life is more than the pebbles in David's hands
I look forward
I see the red sea
I look back
I see the Egyptian chariots
Trapped I feel
The ground unyielding
Firm it stood
It could have swallowed me up
No wings like the eagle
I could have flown with the wind
The tree to provide shelter
Is but a carrier of thorns
The one to blow out dirt from my eyes
Peppered his tongue
But Moses-like
I lift up my eyes
Heavenward and I heard
A voice:
"Child, it's in your hands"

---

* 27-12-2007

57. Is my girl alright?

Solo: *Ero mi r'ojeje*
Chorus: *Ojeje*
Solo: *E ba mi ki Baba mi*
Chorus: *ojeje*
Solo: *Pe eyin to fi sile*
Solo: *Orogun ma mu je*
Solo: *Ewura to kan gogo*

'Travellers to Ojeeje'
Oh, Wayfarers
On the trail to Ojeeje

Without shoes
You trudge on
At the breaking of the new day
Your knees clean off
The dew at dawn
As you move on

May you reach your destination
In one piece
May God make a way for you
His pillar of clouds leads by day
His pillar of light by night

When you arrive
Do tell him who begat me
What fate befalls me
Let him know
That the egg he left
Has become the bitter waterleaf

Let him know
That instead of joy
Cries become my heart
That each night, and
With each day
Mourning becomes the golden girl

But tell him too
That the golden girl is holding on
In prayer, and in praise to God
For a fresh breath of life.

84

58. You are Mad*

I can see the glint in your eyes
Your hair dishevelled
Hands shaking. Restless
Unsettled pupils
Almost dilating
She opens her mouth
Words of wisdom stumble out
Only the thief knows
The footsteps of another on the rock
MAD. DAM. Possessed
Corrupted and crossed
All senses lost
Damned
Damned like the dam of river Niger
Its free flow shut
Heavy, overflowed
No outlet; chocked
Bursting out for air

The sky is heavy
Its pregnant cloud must burst loose
The sane is insane
The supposed insane is saner
For a thin line divides
Sanity from insanity
Or love from hate

---

* 27-12-2007

The teacher, chalk in hand
Cigarette in the other
Hears breaking news
In haste
He inhales the chalk
To the chagrin of his students

What then is ingenuity?
Another name for madness
What is great exploit?
But out of the world feat

Who dares call another mad?
Who casts the first stone?
When his sanity leaves
So much to be desired!

She's mad
She's mad
She eats pounded yam with *isi ewu*
She's mad, she's mad
She eats *amala* with the leg of mutton
She's mad, she's mad
She brought stout-pillars
To your home stead

59. For 27 years

For 27 years, O Lord
For 27 years
I have been comatose
Throttling on half cylinder
Encumbered by strange veil
That darkened the glory You invested in me
Turned into a door mat
The glory becomes the village bowl
In which everyone spits.

Lord, how long will thou look on?
How long will the heathen rage?
And the people imagine a vain thing?
Let my soul escape from the trap

They rage
They bare their teeth
They show their fangs
Ever ready to pounce
The Lord laughs at them
For their time is up

Show up for me
You are the health and strength of my life
Prove Yourself
Defend your name and Your word
You who exalt Your word more than Your name
You said, You will arise with healing in Your wings
Arise for my sake

27 years is a long time
For a child to become a man of his own
Lord, You are the God of all flesh

You said so.
You said;
Ask and I will give the nations to you
I ask;
Put an end to this storm
It's gone on for far too long
Raise a standard against the flood
Let me leap over the troop by Your help
Your praise waits in my mouth.

60. **Arise, O Lord**

Let Your enemies be scattered
Arise in Your power
And in Your strength
Arise with all that makes You, God
Arise and defend Your own

Arise in Your Almightiness
Let Your enemies in my life scatter
Arise and fight my battles
Arise, arise, arise.

As Your child, I ask
You, to stir up thyself from Your throne of grace
Show me mercy
Show me grace
Let favour envelope me
Let Your inexplicable mercy
Your joy unspeakable
Your peace immeasurable
Be my portion

You said: Ask, seek and knock
I ask in prayer
I seek with praises and worship and
I knock in thanksgiving

Arise, O Lord for my sake
Let my accusers know that I serve You
Put a stop to this misery
By Your mercy
Arise for me

61. I roam

I roam and roam
My mind is room enough to roam
I wander up and down
In the crevices of my soul
I search and search
The nooks and crannies
My mind in turmoil;
Howling and thundering
As I toss and turn through the terrified torment of a night to
daybreak
Where is the way out?

No answer to the rescue
As the questions ravaged my soul
My face a constant frown
Bellying the torture of my heart

In helplessness
I yield my all to Him
Having found no succour elsewhere
For only in Him am I fulfilled
As I burst into a song
In praise of my Maker
Who knew me when I was not

I yearn for rest
Away from the difficulties of this darkling plain
Peace is costly here
And I seem not to have the currency
To purchase the peace of the world
In utter despair
When all else failed
I yield my life to Him

Who gives the peace that the world cannot give
He speaks and I am at peace
At His word; I am renewed
From my wanderings and wonderings
He speaks and I bow in reverence
To Him who died and lives again and again

Your peace is enough for me
With You I can never be wrong.

62. In Vain

In vain they dug their hole for my soul
In vain they cast their net for my body
In vain the accusers weave grand tales of deception
In vain they send arrows of evil against me
But all in vain

I am a child of God
Joint heirs with Christ
The word of God my sword
His promises my joy

I am sustained by the Everlasting Arms
His outstretched arms support me
His right hand of righteousness saves
His ear not deaf to hear me
His eyes watch they sparrows
He watches me, more

My God is never late
He saves at the nick of time
While I am yet speaking;
The answer is provided

Why torture me so?
Why molest me sore?
Why send arrows to me?

I am a child of God!
I dwell in Him and He in me
My soul cannot be depressed
My life is in the hollow of His hands
"No power of hell
No scheme of man can ever pluck me from His hands"

No tribulation. No attack
No molestation. No harassment
No divination. No enchantment
No incantation. No delay
Can pluck me from my source

In vain you try
In vain you lose
For Christ in me; the hope of my glory

63. Like a Bear

Like a bear tied to the stake
I fight blindly known and unknown adversaries
Like hunters they surround me with bows and arrows

You had warned: come home early
The consequences are dire
I listened and heard but I forgot
I failed to realise the gravity of those last words
"Come home early..."

I was ill and it happened
I didn't go home

Since then
I had suffered
I had eaten my food as medicine and my medicine as food
That disobedience has been costly
It has taken my peace and joy
The daughter of the butcher has only bones to eat
The daughter of the clothes seller wears rags

I turn my face to the wall
On my knees, in utter desperation
I cry my eyes out

Now, I seek mercy
I call for compassion
I long for divine kindness
Like the prodigal
I desire tender mercies
For I have wasted my years in reckless abandonment

I am back, dear Lord
To the lover of my soul
At Your feet only
To restitute for my wantonness
Make me a candidate of your lovingkindness
In trepidation, I plead
Is there still something You have for this daughter of Zion?
Something to assuage this hurt, this ache and pain?

I know You, Lord
You are full of mercy
Your anger endures but for a moment
You made all
You will not cast me off

I rot in my disobedience to Father
I don't want to be Saul, the king
I would rather be David, the king
A man after Your own heart

Look on me with mercy
Don't watch me suffer endlessly
When I have You
You said, after you have suffered a while…
You will settle me
I know a thousand years is like a day in Your presence
Lord, it's been hell
Don't look on while I suffer
Now is the time to intervene
Let this be the battle that will end all battles.

I know You can

64. Literati a la Ife

To all solid steps
These toddling ones imitate
To transport me into ages of sojourns
When we traverse the world
The Dragon did dance here in my time
For *The Native Son* was in the Carnival.
"As a matter of fact, 'that fellow' remains
Indomitable in espousing 'content and form'"
Content in the last resort determines form … you know -.
Hmh. What with Ezeulu the pumpkin leaf festival
Would not have given way to the Bells present even in the shrine!
Brecht's alienating tactics de-empathise no Umuaroans
Swarming instinctively like flies to the kill.
The stairs up meandering clumsy
Thus I need some 'Emotivity'
To lighten my darkness
The Pragmatological onomatopoeic remains
But its Narratologicalness
Provided another level of conflictualisation
And makes it more Imagistic!
Our friend – 'hegemonic and counter' – hegemonic
You who 'shaka' the occasion exceedingly well.
The character must not be submerged in the action
He definitely must perform
Not just in the Theng'eta session
Since he is no escapist like Munira
No Gogo nor Didi
His is a round, three- dimensional characterisation.
Our friend the poet
Strain yourself no more
The visual aids you employ
Mirror the content perfectly
Your face a book

From where we decode the content.
No room for 'Agbero Bourgeoisie' here
The Urhobo Wayo wades through
Any Poto-poto, anyday, anytime
To enumerate problems of oral literature
Transcending ultimately by providing
Eans of 'technologising' it
Our Udje clansman, we should ask you
What became of 'Oyeghe'
Or was she abducted by Tovotayen?
Our 'Young Good man Brown' deserves
No 'Scarlet Letter'
For the Puritan sensibilities
Must metamorphose eventually into
The meretriciousness of *The Great Gatsby*
But then their dream remains one in a million
Its inimitability sustain the world
From cynicism … You know.
No! The grandmother leaves not her children
No even to recapture the past
The Marabar caves (though) different and numerous
Distinctive yet similar
The same sun and sky cover them
The Gradgrinds' 'hard facts … Nothing but facts'
Would not erode our 'circus' emotion
For imagination is our watchword!
Yes! How can I forget you
The important Egungun that
Emerges last from the Grove (*Igbale*)
Not to chant Jodughatu-song
But like Folumo; the warrior-cleanser masquerade
Infuses vitality into the dance
The cockerel dances not without its feathers
Like Africa carrying the world on her shoulder
Like the canoe pole
Stirring the river into action.

We hope women will not be
Made to kneel at Agemo any longer
Or is it a question of
'*We wo fere, we kufere*!
Ours is no caricature
No type, No phegmatism
Here there is no flatness
No purveyor of melodrama.
The Recipe is simple;
Take the verbal; content and Ideology
Add style; not all style and no content here
Stir vigorously with physiognomacy; its kinesics
Sprinkle liberally with intense enthusiasm
Simmer with regular adequate lectures.
My Grub thus flavoured and curried
Washes down the throat
Nourishing not only
The HEAD but the HEART

To all solid steps
These toddling ones
Imitate.

65. All My Eggs in God's Basket*

Do not put all your eggs in one basket;
The world tells me
But I haven't got any eggs
That wasn't given by God
The world says "diversify"
That's the key
I say "in Him alone I trust"
"All other ground is sinking sand"
The elders say "what if this your way leads to failure"
I retort "there is only one way"
Narrow and straight that leads to fullness of joy
It is risky to face "a way"
Try other ways
When one fails you have another
I reason "all my eggs in God's basket"
I may be "tempest tossed"
My anchor remains firm
With God, there is no failure!
With my eggs in His basket
I have nothing to fear on a rough road
I sleep in the storm, unshaken
In Him, I find rest
The storm may rage
The winds may howl
The trees bow to the powerful howling
The whirlwind rouse the sleepy dust from its slumbering
The rain beat the roofs in anger
My eggs remain engravened in the palm of His hands
Because I made a choice;
To put all my eggs in His basket

---

* 23-02-2022

66. The Prophecy

She will steal
She will lie
She will sleep with even a dog

He is clean
He is perfect
The head

Take Her.
No! Face contorted at the sight of the riddle

Oruku tindi tindi
It is a riddle wrapped in an enigma
Oruku tindi tindi

Keep her to your bosom
Like Mary and her Lamb
You go;
She follows

If you can
You are free
You and your generations
Born and unborn
Cast in this sea of life

Like the gardener
He sets about his task
Digging,
Planting
Watering
Tendering
Manuring

Opekete n dagba
Inu adamo n baje
The young palm tree grows
The watcher begrudges

They watched
They waited

But he gave his life
For her
He loses his life
That he may regain it
In her.

67. Too Many Times*

Too many times, I force my way
Too many times, I assert myself
Too many times, I fix things
And too many times, I fail

In solitude, I recollect in pain
I see that "by strength shall no man prevail"
I realise not too late
To bow to God's power

I am forced by recognise that He sees the bigger picture
He knows the end from the beginning
He is stronger than the strongest
Why then do I strive and fight as one that beat the wind?

Lord, I bow to Your majesty
I yield in total surrender
To the one who knew me before I was conceived in my mother's womb
The One who didn't allow childhood diseases wrench me from my mother
The One who has been there to my Ebenezer

I find out, not too late
That I shouldn't fight without my mighty warrior

Lord, I cannot see my way
Be my light
I am too weak

---

* 23-02-2022

Be my strength
I walk in the shadow of death
Be my confidence
I cannot be who You designed me to be
Be my guide

I am not running ahead of You, again
I am not running to a mountain or to any hill
I am not running from pillar to post
I seek no dream and vision from charlatans
I do not chase shadows
I no longer grope in darkness
As I wait for instruction
From my Designer

68. Immobile

I cannot move forward
Going back is impossible
The elders say "when going forward is impossible, retrace your
steps"
Here am I transfixed at Point Jesus
Rooted to the spot; I give in
 Your will is my command.

I wait on You, with all I have
In prayer
In supplication
In praises
Denying life's pleasures
I wait on You.

Life like an escalator takes me up and down
My eyes clouded with tears that I cannot see my way
My pillow drenched each night with a deluge of tears
Friends becomes foes in the market of life
As we tear one another up with tales of deceit
Alone, I turn to You
No one to trust with a thought
No shoulder to lean on a dreary and weary night.

But You are true
Unchanging in Your immeasurable love for me
You have rescued me before
Now isn't the time to fail
Come true and through for me

69. Ikoyi Road

The land is vast
The atmosphere serene
The quietness almost absolute
The grass is green and luscious
The buildings old and dreary; yet they welcome us
No floods here
Streets paved to the entrance
The murky gutters well hidden behind concrete slabs
Trees sing, bowing and wave Halleluyah in the rain
I sighed and purred in contentment;
This is what my heart craves

But all is a façade
For the misery it hides
Every woman's fear

Come to the window, my love
Hear the birds on the lintel chirruping all day long without a care
My grandmother heard this misery long ago
Alone like a hen she raised her brood
With an absent father
My mother escaped it
Father was a man of one-wife

Come to the window, my love
Behold the beauty of the land
It recommends itself to our senses

I had faith
That this was life-long

Come to the window
Together, we enjoy the coolness of this place

He did not answer
I looked back, in haste
He wasn't there again

My faith has been shaken
I thought we could live till grey and hoary hairs
Together, holding ourselves, drinking in our own embrace
But now I only see his withdrawing back
Staring me in the face
If only we were true to each other
"The world which seems to lie before us like a land of dreams"
So serene, so beautiful, giving us hope
Does not care for our soul surviving
Now we are at crossroads
Swept by tales of betrayal and accusations and counter-accusations
Ignorant of our future.

70. The Piglet.*

The piglet asks its mother
Mother, why is your mouth big and ugly?
The sow stopped in her stride, deep in thought
Hmmmmmmm. When matter gets to the issue of a tail
The frog suggests we forget the matter

Finally, she grunted
Never worry, son
The things my eyes have seen
The burden my body has borne
The rain that had fallen on my bare back
The child who berates its father for being poor
Let's see how it ends

Child, tell me, after some seasons
Why your mouth is like mine.

_____

* 30-11-**2021**

107

71. The rain's been on for far too long

It has been raining since March, 1995
When father left this side of the divide
There have been glimmers of sunshine
Quickly covered by clouds of uncertainties and sorrow
From one house of healing to another
From emotional trauma to vituperations.

When rain falls, it sure stops
Even Noah's flood subsided and found dry land
Lord, it's been raining for too long
End this torrent, O Lord
It has destroyed the farms
Famine is real here
It has caused deep gullies
A deep gash opens on the road
Nothing has been able to stand in the way of this heavy ceaseless
downpour

In it all
There is a small house of faith
As small as a mustard seed
Anchored on a rock
Standing unmoved, unshaken
The lightning flashed against it
The thunder boomed on it hitting at its foundations
But it stood
The roof bear holes as tales of its buffeting

The stronger house peeped at this inconsequential mustard seed
house
And wonder why it is still standing
Many saw avenues to afflict her
She has no one to defend her

They see what she cannot see
They pull and tug at her being; her foundation
They hear her prayers like howling amidst the storm
They peep through the thundering and wonder why she howls so
The mustard seed house opens her heart to her Maker
"You made others big and strong, bright and beautiful.
You made me too, in my minuteness for Your pleasure!
Even in this torrential rain
I pour my love on You
Let it rise up with sweet smelling savour unto You
Let the fragrance of Your love envelope me"

The big houses with fenced walls heard the praises of God
"Shut up, already" Can't you see yourself?
He can't hear you
You are a nuisance here
You are too inconsequential
He has greater things to deal with
Shut up, we are trying to sleep
Give in
Give up
Let the tide sweep you away
No one would even notice
Just surrender to the pull of the swellings and ride easily to your
end
It is easy
Give in to the power of the pouring"

She blocked her ears to the rantings
And kept at praising her God
"I want to live for You
My dead body cannot praise You in the grave
My life will bring You pleasure"

Her eyes like windows to her heart well up with tears
Her mouth like doors open in spite of the pain

To declare God's awesome greatness and mercy
She tells of His unconditional, immeasurable loving kindness and
tender mercies
That birthed Jesus, Saviour of the world
The mustard seed house sang of His presence even in the flood of
live

And like it came upon the earth surreptitiously
It fizzled out, the torrential unceasing storm
It was as if it was never there at all
The clouds clear up
The sun appears unsure from its hiding place
The floods dry up
The earth resumes its chores
The big houses look to the mountain
Lo, there stood the mustard seed house, glimmeringly,
Unmoved.
Her foundation in God was sure and steady

Lightning Source UK Ltd.
Milton Keynes UK
UKHW040613031022
409831UK00001B/42